P9-DGC-418

THOMAS A. CANTORE
417 HOMESTEAD DR.
UTICA, NY 13502

Photograph © 1981 by John Wetterman

MY 55 WAYS

O LOWER YOUR GOLF SCORE

by Jack Nicklaus

with drawings by Francis Golden

A FIRESIDE BOOK
Published by Simon & Schuster, Inc.
New York

Copyright © 1962, 1963, 1964 by Jack Nicklaus

All rights reserved
including the right of reproduction
in whole or in part in any form

First Fireside Edition, 1985

Published by Simon & Schuster, Inc.
Simon & Schuster Building
Rockefeller Center
1230 Avenue of the Americas
New York, New York 10020

FIRESIDE and colophon are registered trademarks
of Simon & Schuster, Inc.
Designed by Helen Barrow

Manufactured in the United States of America

10 9 8 7 6 5 4 3 2 1
10 9 8 7 6 5 4 3   Pbk.

Library of Congress Cataloging in Publication Data

Nicklaus, Jack.
    My 55 ways to lower your golf score.

    Reprint. Originally published: New York, N.Y.: Simon
and Schuster, c1964. With new introd.
    "A Fireside book."
    1. Golf. I. Title. II. Title: My fifty-five ways to
lower your golf score.
GV965.N5   1985   796.352'3   84-23552

ISBN 0-671-55746-7
ISBN 0-671-55395-X Pbk.

CONTENTS

FOREWORD

Golf has been a very important part of my life ever since I first began swatting a ball around the back yard with a set of sawed-off clubs. I can remember my grim determination, at about the age of six, to learn to hit the golf ball clear over the garage—at the time a seemingly impossible task. Practice was the only answer. As any golf professional will tell you, the learning process in this game does not by any means begin and end on the fairway or on a practice tee. While practice is the most beneficial method of improving your game, it is not enough to work continually on a variety of golf shots. There must be careful planning. You may be practicing some bad habits. Thus, it is just as important to think about the intricacies of your swing, consider various strategies, review each day's game or practice, and evaluate your performance as critically as possible, both before and after a practice session.

By the time I reached junior high school, I had pretty much decided to make golf a career and to become as fine a player as possible. This decision meant complete devotion to the game, and I can recall many lonely, and sometimes frustrating, hours on the practice tee, in good weather and bad, trying to attain my goal. I discussed the game with my dad, local golf professionals and literally anyone in the area willing to analyze the execution of various shots. I studied the swings of the better golfers in Ohio and always looked forward to watching the touring professionals in action. In addition, I began to fill my library with every instructional golf book I could find. Believe me, there have been many such books written during the past fifty years by a variety of authors, from the professionals to other self-styled experts.

Almost every book made some claim to revealing the "secret of golf," or of being able to correct any and every flaw which plagued the reader at the time. To be perfectly honest, some of the books were helpful on occasion, but a good many of them simply added sometimes to my own confusion. One major drawback of most books was a distinct lack of proper illustration. The old adage about a picture's being worth a thousand words may be a bit shopworn, but it is certainly appropriate to the field of instructional golf booklets. I can remember practically contorting myself in an effort to follow what was supposed to be a simple description of the way to correct a particular fault.

While still in college, I had no particular ambitions about writing a golf book, nor did I ever delude myself into thinking I could solve anyone's golf problems better than those who had tried before. I do remember forming a definite opinion as to the contents of an instructional golf book, and deciding that one excellent method would be well-drawn pictures and diagrams with as simple an explanation as possible in narrative form.

After turning professional and joining the "golf circuit" in 1962, I was given the opportunity to write a series of articles for Sports Illustrated. *In agreeing to undertake this task, I insisted upon two major considerations. First, I was to be given sufficient time to discuss each article at great length with the magazine's editorial consultant, retaining complete control and right of approval over both picture and narrative. Second, and most important, I wanted an artist who knew the game of golf and who could spend plenty of time with me simply sitting down and discussing the mechanics of golf. This sort of conference helped me as much as the artist. A tape recorder was used to great advantage in capturing a whole session of this "shop talk." In addition, we used many rolls of film taking motion pictures.*

I was gratified to learn that what started out as a brief ten-part series of instruction was so well received by golfing enthusiasts that it blossomed into a regular feature of the magazine and now has become this book. I looked forward to planning these articles and we began experimenting with different techniques of emphasizing certain aspects of a particular golf swing. For example, we used different colors to vividly illustrate a sequence with just one basic picture. We also used varying colors to emphasize such things as a firm grip, creation of power with the right leg, starting the swing downward with the proper muscles, and calling attention to common mistakes. We also found that a series of arrows, properly placed, could be extremely helpful. I was amazed to discover that such arrows, in conjunction with the picture, could literally describe the proper actions themselves, making a long explanation unnecessary.

As you will discover in reading this book, we made no concerted effort to begin at one starting point with fundamentals and continue through in a schematic form. Rather, we decided simply to reproduce an entire series, almost at random, but touching at some point upon literally every type of golf shot or situation.

You may or may not find any "secrets" in these pages or in the diagrams. That is not the intention of the book. On the other hand, what I hope you will find are some good, solid fundamentals set forth in a manner which is not only intelligible, but which will also emphasize the points I have found to be important.

No one who has ever whacked a good drive down the middle, or who has drilled in a 30-foot birdie putt, needs to be told what a great game golf really is. It is sometimes more difficult to look upon the game in such gleeful satisfaction when too many shots roll off into the rough, or when you are counting the score of each hole with an adding machine. I hope that this book, just by stressing fundamentals, will be of some help to everyone, regardless of handicap. But it is not keyed to any one group, nor is it directed toward beginners. The book was written with the intention of reaching anyone interested enough to want to think a little more about the game.

Finally, one word of caution. This book may not always set forth what you have recognized to be the generally accepted principles of a golf swing. The only methods I have attempted to convey are my own. For that reason, you need not accept all the described techniques. On the other hand, the methods pictured and described in this book have brought me at least a fair degree of success, and on that basis ought to be worth a try. If there were not an infinite number of ways to score well in this game, it would not be nearly so fascinating. If the game required no thought, it would not be interesting at all. Therefore, the least I can hope for is that this book will make you think about your swing—and that in itself should make the game more rewarding for you.

—JACK NICKLAUS

Get distance first,
control later

A long backswing helps develop the muscles of the left leg, for they are quite active during a full body turn.

It has long been thought that the proper way to teach children to play golf is to insist that they learn a careful, deliberate swing first,

A full pivot and follow-through strengthen the right leg, because the muscles must push very hard into the shot.

then strive for distance. But I feel that just the opposite is correct. The first thing I learned was to swing hard, and never mind where the ball went. That is the way Arnold Palmer was taught, too, and I think it is the right way. A youngster first trying golf will enjoy the game more if allowed to whale away at the ball, and he will be developing the muscles he needs to become a strong hitter. Once he has achieved distance, he can learn control while still hitting a long ball. An especially important factor in distance hitting is leg strength. Learning to swing by combining a full body turn with a long backswing will help develop the left leg. A full pivot on the downswing, combined with a full follow-through, requires a firm push-off with the right leg and will help strengthen it. If a golfer does this while young he will get the leg strength needed to hit very long shots. I know that my distance is due more to the strength in my legs than to any power I might be getting from my arms, hands or fingers.

Give every shot
a cockeyed look

Tournament spectators will notice that a great many touring pros turn their heads to the right just before starting the backswing, an action that is especially marked in myself and Sam Snead. This cocking of the head is something more than just a nervous twitch. It serves three valuable purposes. First, it is a positive move, like the forward press of the hands, from which to start the backswing. Second, turning the head to the right makes it possible to take a longer, freer turn with the whole body than would be possible if the head were held straight to the front. Third, and most important, it is a method by which we help brace ourselves against swaying to the left on the downswing and moving our body out ahead of the ball at impact—a sure way to ruin a golf swing.

Cocking the head can cause one problem. A player whose strong, or master, eye is his right one may be bothered at first by finding his nose somewhat in his line of vision to the ball. But one eye on the ball is enough. The advantages of cocking the head outweigh the disadvantage.

Cocking the head should be the last thing you do before starting the backswing. Take your normal stance (left), then, just before moving the club, turn your head to the right.

The hips should rotate through the swing like a revolving cylinder. On the backswing, concentrate on turning the right hip away from the ball until the left hip and the shoulder (green dot) are even with it or behind it.

On the downswing and the follow-through the emphasis should be on turning the right hip toward the ball and the hole. If the right hip is rotating properly, the rest of the body turn will follow almost automatically.

Think about one hip and they both will turn correctly

If you are pushing your shots to the right instead of hitting them long and straight, look to the hip turn as the likely trouble spot. You may

find that you have restricted yourself because of an improper hip turn on the backswing, and on the downswing are "sliding" your hips laterally toward the target instead of turning them. Both faults will occur at the expense of power and accuracy. The following remedies can often get you back in the right groove. Most of us are right-handed, and it is often easier for us to think in right-handed terms. On the backswing, therefore, concentrate specifically on turning the right hip away from the ball, rather than just generally turning both hips. The result is the same, but thinking of it this way makes the movement seem less complicated and therefore easier to accomplish correctly. Be sure to turn the right hip so far that the left hip and left shoulder have also rotated enough to be opposite or behind the ball. While you are doing this your weight will shift back to the right foot. On the downswing, concentrate on turning the right hip toward the ball. This will force the left hip out of the way, not "slide" it laterally to the left. Incorrectly sliding the left side toward the target will reduce the speed of the swing and get the hands ahead of the ball at impact, making a pushed shot inevitable. If on the follow-through the front of the body, not the left side, is squarely facing the target, it is likely you have made a proper hip turn and pivot. It is difficult to say exactly when the weight should move off the right foot and onto the left, but I feel that my weight begins shifting to the left the instant my hips start turning to the left.

The hips should turn so far that the front of the body is pointing straight toward the target as the follow-through is completed.

On the backswing (above) the left knee pushes in and the body coils around the right knee, which is tightly locked. On the downswing (right) the right knee releases all of this pent-up power.

Knee action for a power play

One of the most overlooked sources of power in a golf swing is the knees, especially the right knee. The hips, knees and feet all work together in creating power, but the knees serve as the focal point. Here are a few things to consider on the practice tee if you are not getting the distance you think you should. For every shot except the very short ones, a line extending across the kneecaps should point at the target. As the club comes back, the left knee should turn in toward the right. Now the right knee becomes the critical point of the entire swing. It should be locked in position and not move at all during the backswing. When it is braced in this fashion, the body is coiling like a spring around the knee. This firmness builds up power for the downswing. It also makes it impossible to lose power by swaying away from the ball. As the downswing starts, the strength contained by the right knee is abruptly released by pushing off the inside of the right foot. This will cause the right knee to turn directly toward the target, which helps push the whole body, and the power in it, in the direction the ball is being hit. One word of caution. Before you look for such a source of additional power, you must have a well-disciplined basic swing.

When the swing is finished, the right knee faces the hole.

Some tricks
that will cheat the wind

There are two basic principles to keep in mind on those days when the wind is threatening to destroy your poise and your game. If the wind is in your face you should hit a shot that imparts very little backspin to the ball. If the wind is at your back you should concentrate on getting the ball up into the air as fast as you possibly can.

The best way to reduce backspin on a shot directly into the wind is to play the ball back nearer the right foot than usual, while keeping the hands in the same relative position to the ball that they would normally be at address—if the ball has been moved back two inches, move the hands back two inches. The result will be a shot that will start low, stay low and have little backspin. The same technique should be employed regardless of what club is used. However, on an iron shot, depending on the strength of the wind, the player should drop down two or three clubs (a four-iron, for instance, in place of a six) and hit the shot very softly.

Getting the ball up fast for a downwind shot can be achieved by playing the ball well forward—actually off the left foot—and keeping the right shoulder below the left throughout most of the swing. The right arm and hand are the dominating features of the swing. Generally, a downwind shot can be hit quite hard without too much danger, because the wind will tend to straighten out either a hook or a slice.

The straight line usually formed by the arm and club shaft must be altered for a shot into the wind.

The fact that only about one-third of the players on the pro tour carry a one-iron in their bags need not discourage many amateurs from doing so. If you are strong enough to hit two- and three-irons consistently well (in other words, able to hit down on the ball with a shallow-faced club hard enough to get it into the air) you should certainly consider the one-iron. This is especially true if you tend to be wild with fairway woods. The one-iron is an excellent driving club on tight holes. With it you get about the same distances as with a four-wood, but at the same time you can expect much more accuracy and control. It is also a good club to use when hitting into the wind. It keeps the ball low, and therefore is more likely to keep the shot on line than a fairway wood. It will also carry further than a four-wood against the wind. Finally, a one-iron produces more backspin than most wood shots, which is important when hitting to small greens.

But here are some warnings: forget the one-iron anytime you are having trouble with other long irons; never try to use the one-iron from a tight lie; remember that you are allowed to carry only 14 clubs.

The face of the one-iron has less loft than the four-wood—as the bars (right) show—so one-irons are easier to control under certain conditions.

f the longest iron

3-IRON   2-IRON   1-IRON   4-WOOD

The tempo of the swing

Many golfers, touring pro and weekend player alike, are so concerned with the mechanics of the grip and the swing that they often overlook an important element of good golf: tempo or rhythm. By tempo or rhythm I mean the rate at which the club is taken back and then brought down into the ball. The two phases of the swing, the backswing and the downswing, should be carried out at pretty much the same tempo. The clubhead will always travel much faster coming down than going back, but the hands will not. Thus they should establish the tempo. If you have a fast backswing the downswing should also be fairly fast, otherwise you will lose momentum and therefore distance. If your backswing is slow and the downswing too fast you are likely to lose control of the club at the top of the swing and thus have trouble hitting the ball straight. So work at maintaining a uniform speed.

Another consideration is whether the present speed of your swing is right for you. Maybe you employ a slow, leisurely tempo when a fast one would work more effectively. Or vice versa. You must find the tempo best suited for you, and you will not find it by guesswork. You must learn how fast you can take the club back and still maintain momentum, balance and control on the downswing. Instead of being satisfied with the tempo you are now using—after all, who is ever satisfied with his golf game—why not experiment on the practice tee to see if a change in tempo improves your shots?

The tempo on the backswing and the downswing should be close to that of a metronome.

If despite a smooth, strong swing you are not getting the distance you feel you deserve, it may well be because your hip-turn through the hitting zone is too restricted. I have made two adjustments at address to overcome this restriction. I think the changes have given me freedom to move my hips faster on the downswing, increasing my distance as much as 10%, and I recommend them. At address most golfers will turn the left foot about 30° to the left. When I tried this particular stance I always felt that my hip turn was being checked too soon and that as a consequence I was losing power. My left foot is now turned out 45°. In addition, I have moved my right foot forward just a little so that my stance is a slightly open one, rather than closed as is more conventional. Thus I am set up like a boxer who is about to throw a long right-hand punch and who must get his body completely out of the way if he expects to hit his opponent hard. On the down-swing I am able, like the boxer, to achieve a fuller turn with my hips as well as to develop much more body leverage behind the ball at impact. With these adjustments I now feel sure that every ounce of my body is being utilized in hitting the shot.

The right foot (red) is placed farther forward than usual, thus creating an open stance that aims to the left of target (red line) instead of to the right.

To gain additional power, turn your left foot a little more toward the hole at address than is conventional (as shown in red outline above). The foot should be turned out at about 45° instead of at the customary 30°.

A slight fade off the tee keeps
the ball in play

To eliminate any chance of a hook, the right hand should move straight out toward the target (arrow) at and after impact, not roll over (dotted line).

Every time you play golf you are going to encounter narrow holes, where accuracy off the tee is far more important than distance. Since a dead-straight shot is one of the hardest to hit and a hook can often get completely out of control, accuracy is best achieved with a controlled fade. Such a shot can be hit by doing what is called blocking out. The phrase refers to the right side and the right hand, which are blocked from dominating the shot, making a hook impossible.

The swing for the controlled fade should be made primarily with the arms. The backswing must be all arms, compact and smooth, with very little wrist action. The downswing must not be forced. At impact it is necessary that the left side remain rigid and that the right hand move straight out toward the target, neither getting ahead of the left hand nor rolling over it. The follow-through should be high and upright.

If the trouble on the hole is to the left, the shot should be aimed right at it. The ball should fade some 20 yards from left to right, thus moving away from the trouble zone. If the hazards are on the right, the shot has another advantage: it doesn't roll far. If it lands on the fairway it is likely to stay there.

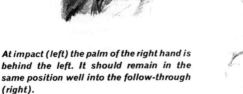

At impact (left) the palm of the right hand is behind the left. It should remain in the same position well into the follow-through (right).

The hands come from inside the ball (left),
and the right shoulder stays underneath the
left after impact (right).

A player attempting an intentional hook should not rely on a strong grip and a closed stance alone to produce the desired effect. They are simply not enough. In fact, the most vital element lies in the execution itself, in keeping the right shoulder underneath the left as the hands and clubhead go out through the ball. This action— provided the other adjustments have been made—will not only produce a hook, but a hook that will stay under control and land softly.

You should begin by picking a spot, say a tree or bush, to the right of your target. Align your stance and square the club face to this aiming point. Play the ball in the normal position but adjust your grip, turning the hands slightly more to the right than usual. This will help the right hand to roll over at impact, producing hook spin. On the downswing make sure that your head stays absolutely still. Your hands come from inside the ball, the right shoulder stays underneath the left and the hands go out toward the preliminary target and finish high. To recreate the feeling of how the shot should be executed, visualize a softball pitcher throwing an underhand pitch toward the plate.

The intentional hook

For a low, hooked long-iron shot, I play my ball nearer my right foot than usual, and hit down through it with a quick roll of my wrists.

There are numerous occasions, but particularly on windy days, when golfers need both the length of a fairway wood and the control that only a long iron can give. When conditions are right the low, hooked long iron can be effective in achieving this combination. By proper conditions I mean a hard or firm fairway that will offer plenty of roll and a green that is not fronted by hazards.

The second hole at Pebble Beach in California is a good example from my competitive experience. It is also the type of hole I see pretty often on the winter tour. It is a 480-yard par 5. The fairway is firm, and the green, which is firm too, is not trapped directly in front. A high-flying fairway wood shot would be risky, because of a steady wind that sweeps across the hole. Also, the green is backed by an out-of-bounds and is too firm to hold a long-approach hit directly into it.

The first time I played the hole during the Crosby in 1962 I used a long iron for my second shot and hit a low hook under the wind. For this type of shot I always play the ball back nearer my right foot than normally and aim to the right of the target. I bring the clubhead down through the ball very hard, rolling my wrists quickly during impact. You can count on the hard fairway, the low trajectory and the great amount of overspin to give you 10 to 15 more yards than a long iron ordinarily would supply. Because of these factors I was able to roll the ball right up onto the green during that round at the Crosby and then knocked in the putt for an eagle 3.

nd true with the long irons

To avoid choking up,

try choking down

When you reach that tense point at which you need only put an approach shot into the middle of the 18th green and two-putt to break 80 or take a Nassau or win the club championship, you should be able to hit what the touring professionals unblushingly call the choke stroke. It involves, first, some mental decisions. You should figure out what side of the green has the most hazards around it and then resolve to favor the other side. You should decide what type of shot you feel most confident of being able to hit cleanly—a fade or a hook, low or high—and then set yourself up to hit that type of shot. If you have been fading your irons a little all day, do not try to change. Assume the shot will fade. Let it fade. Because you are under physical as well as emotional tension, you are going to grip the club more tightly than normal, swing it faster than usual and, very likely, raise up off the ball a little. This will give you somewhat more distance and less backspin than you would like. So allow for it. Choke down on the club more than you normally would. Start the backswing more slowly than usual and then swing down into the ball as if simply punching it off the turf. By doing this you are making compensations for the likely extra distance and speedier swing, and you are fairly sure of getting the shot at least off and headed for the target.

When the tension is high and a par is needed, the ball should be punched toward the green's safe side (green shading) and well away from any possible danger zone (red).

When a long blast is required,
dig in deep

After my first tour on the pro circuit and plenty of time spent in observation, experimentation and practice, I finally got the knack of a shot that is quite difficult for most golfers. This is the long, full iron from a fairway sand trap. The problem is that you are not only hitting from a sandy lie but that your feet are likely to slip while you are trying to make the shot. The very first point to check is how much loft you will need to clear any mound at the front of the trap. Next, if clearing the edges of the trap will be no problem, select a club one number longer than you would ordinarily use (a two-iron, say, instead of a three-iron). Choke up on the club. This not only gives better control but compensates for the fact that standing in sand has brought you closer to the ball. After you have addressed the ball, take as full a practice swing as you can to make sure that your feet are solidly planted. It is especially important that your right foot not slip. In hitting, take a slightly more upright swing, and instead of aiming at the back of the ball, concentrate on the top of the ball. You can be almost certain of solid contact this way. The natural loft of the club will get the ball into the air. There have been many times since when I was very thankful I had worked on this shot. During the third round of the 1962 Doral Open, for instance, I was playing in a threesome with Arnold Palmer and Bill Casper and had moved into contention for the lead. On the 14th hole, a 419-yard par 4, I drove into a fairway trap on the left. I choked up on a two-iron, hit the ball out as I have described above and onto the green for a par. This enabled me to finish the round tied with Casper, just one shot out of the lead.

In a fairway trap, choke up on the grip, plant the right foot firmly, and hit strongly through the shot (left). Concentrate on the top of the ball (right).

Longer clubs
won't help a tall golfer

The temptation for a tall player to buy extra-long clubs is a great one. He feels that since he is standing farther from the ball than the average golfer he should also use clubs that are longer than normal. I do not agree with this analysis. Because of the naturally longer arc of his swing, a tall golfer using an unusually long club will be putting too much stress on his ability to control such a big swing. After all, the farther you stand from the ball the harder it is to hit. The most effective club adjustment that can be made is not in the length of the shaft but in the club's degree of uprightness. The taller a man is, the steeper the angle at which the shaft should enter the club head. With clubs that are the conventional length, but more upright, the tall player will be able to place the sole of the clubhead flat on the ground, as it should be, and still stand close enough to the ball to control the shot.

Conversely, a short golfer should not try to use short clubs but should, instead, try a set designed for a flatter swing. This enables him to put the ball farther away from him and thus increase the arc of his swing. Gary Player, who is only 5 feet 7, actually uses a shaft one inch longer than most of the pros on the tour. He finds that this extra shaft length regains the distance his small size tends to cost him, yet does not affect his accuracy. Gary is able to maintain his straightness — granting his excellent swing — because the extra length of his club does not make the arc of his swing too big.

It is the angle that the shaft makes with the clubhead which determines the suitability of clubs. The short man (above) needs clubs with a wider angle than the tall man (right). Note that the clubs themselves are the same length, but the short man has the ball farther away.

Getting a line–

ON THE PRACTICE TEE: Aiming at a target is easy if you can lay the club on the ground, line your feet up with its shaft and have the ball at right angles to this pointer.

One of the most important elements of an effective golf swing is getting the correct alignment. If you are aimed properly you can usually hit the ball fairly straight, even when your swing is mediocre. If you do not get lined up properly the greatest swing in the world will be no good to you, because you will not even be able to guess where the ball will go the next time you hit it.

Getting the right alignment is easy enough on the practice tee. You place a club on the ground, aim it at your target and adjust your stance to the line indicated by the club on the ground. In competition, however, this would be a violation of the golf rule that states no mark shall be placed on the line of play (Rule 9-2), so correcting a faulty alignment can become a problem. What I sometimes do is stand behind the ball and look over it at the target I am trying to hit, be it the green or a spot in the fairway. Then, still standing behind the ball, I square the face of the club to the target. Next, holding the club steady in that position, I walk around it until I am in the proper address position. I can now adjust my stance according to the position of the club face and be confident that I am aiming at the target.

Many golfers are unaware of the effect alignment can have on their game. The next time you find yourself hitting the ball first to the left and then to the right without any apparent reason, check your alignment before you try to adjust any more complicated phase of your game.

ON THE COURSE: *In actual play—since a club cannot be put on the line—you set the club face square to the target, then take your stance without moving the club face.*

The upright swing

A golf swing that emphasizes the use of the arms and minimizes the hands and wrists is the swing most likely to keep the ball in play hole after hole. Anyone strong enough or big enough to be able to get adequate distance with this kind of swing should certainly try it. In the long run it will bring him lower scores. I feel, for instance, that I do nothing more than swing the left arm back, then down, then out through the ball. That is almost all there is to it. There is, of course, a slight bit of hand action — or rolling of the wrists — but this is kept at an absolute minimum. When the wrists are rolled severely on the backswing it also means that the club face is turning well off line. It therefore becomes that much more difficult to bring the club face back absolutely straight at impact. The good arm swing should also be an upright swing. This is achieved by a full body and shoulder turn that starts as soon as the arms begin swinging the club back. The left shoulder should turn well under the chin. Meanwhile, the back of the left hand is kept absolutely square to the line of the swing right up until the hands begin to reach the shoulder level. At this point a certain degree of wrist cocking must take place. This will bring the hands into an upright position at the top of the backswing, from where they can bring the club down with a good deal of power while still keeping the club face — and therefore the ball — on line toward the hole.

The left arm should dominate completely in the upright swing (large drawing), with wrist and hand action kept to a minimum. Even in a full swing with the driver (small drawing) the position of the hands remains the same.

A good time to take a nip,
not a divot

The ball should be played off the left heel (left). At impact (right) the clubhead is just short of the lowest point in the swing.

A common mistake that many golfers make when using a long or medium iron is to try and take a divot — driving the clubhead abruptly down through the ball as if hitting a short iron. Attempting this will usually produce one of three unfortunate consequences: you may hit far behind the ball and barely budge it along the fairway; you may go down through the ball but not be firm enough with your hands, so the ball goes over the green; and you may hit too high on the ball. The best way to eliminate all these errors is simply to sweep the ball off the grass

with the clubhead, striking it just a fraction of an inch before the club-head reaches the lowest point of the swing. Hitting the ball in this manner greatly increases the chance for a shot that will finish some-where on or around the green. To play the shot this way, the ball at address should be positioned opposite the left heel, not back in the center of the stance where so many golfers place it. Then take your regular swing. Forget about the ball. Concentrate, instead, on nipping off the top of the grass that is directly underneath it.

There is no need for panic
in a fairway trap

You have driven into a fairway sand trap and are not only some distance from the green, but also have a poor lie. What can be done? Well, first, stay calm, for you have not necessarily lost a stroke. Assume that you are a seven-iron distance from the green, but the difficult lie indicates that it would be impossible to reach it with that club. Provided the lip of the trap will not interfere, use a five-iron and hit what amounts to a long explosion shot. Play the ball in its normal position between the feet, making sure you have a good firm stance in the sand so that you will not slip during the swing. Open the face of the club and take it back slightly to the outside, using a full backswing. Aim toward the left of the target, because you will be hitting a fading shot, and hit just as close behind the ball as the sand will permit. Hit hard with the right hand, but do not let the wrists turn over at or just after impact. A five-iron explosion hit in this fashion is going to carry approximately as far as a normal seven- or eight-iron shot.

This shot can be played with all the iron clubs, of course, just as long as you remember to use a club two numbers lower than you would normally hit. What's more, you can also get surprisingly good results, provided you are far enough from the green, by hitting the shot with a four-wood. The four-wood has a lot of clubhead weight and passes easily through sand. Employ the same backswing and the same cutting action I have described above, with the right hand controlling the club as it hits the ball. Your friends may think you have lost your mind, walking into a sand trap with a wood, but the shot is not nearly as difficult as it seems.

Before hitting a long explosion from a trap, the feet should be thoroughly dug in, especially along the instep. The club face is opened fairly wide (as shown in the red area) before the backswing starts.

Try using a four-wood from heavy rough

One of the maxims that golf conservatives most honor goes: always use an iron out of the rough. But, quite aside from the fact that it is sometimes wise to gamble, there are many occasions when a four-wood actually is the best club for such a shot. Where the grass is thick this club, used correctly, can do a much better job than an iron. It is a relatively heavy-headed club and has plenty of loft. It will, therefore, cut through even deep grass without being thrown off line. In fact, the four-wood seems almost to have been designed for this kind of rugged work.

When playing such a wood shot stand slightly closer to the ball than is usual. The main problem is to allow as little grass as possible to get between the club face and the ball at impact. The solution lies in taking the club back rather abruptly and hitting down sharply into the ball, but with a full follow-through, thus almost exploding the ball out. This shot will usually slide off to the right a little, so aim slightly to the left. The four-wood can even be used profitably in the rough well inside the club's normal distance, provided you choke up on the grip. Also keep in mind that any ball coming out of high grass will have lots of overspin, and therefore will roll a long way. This makes it possible to reach some holes that might not have been within normal four-wood range.

The ball must be played closer to the feet than usual (top) and the club swung back on an upright plane as if driving stakes with a sledgehammer (bottom).

When confronted with a long-iron approach shot that must clear bunkers or hazards directly in front of the green, the majority of golfers will drill away with all they've got and hope for the best. The trouble with this is that the ball usually will run a long way when it hits. It often bounces into more trouble behind the green than it could have gotten into in front of the green.

The best way to solve this difficult problem is to select a slightly longer iron than is seemingly needed, and then hit a high fade with it. If the distance to the green would ordinarily require a three-iron, a two-iron should be used instead. The ball should be played opposite

ite with the long iron

The ball is played farther to the left and the swing is on a lower plane (red lines) than usual (dotted blue lines).

the left instep, rather than the heel. The club face should be somewhat open at address and, since the ball will fade, it must be aimed to the left of the target. The clubhead is brought straight back, close to the ground. The downswing should be made along much the same trajectory, the clubhead sweeping the ball off the turf instead of hitting down on it. To avoid topping the shot, concentrate on keeping the clubhead low and behind the ball at impact so that it hits the back of the ball and then goes firmly through toward the hole. One word of warning. Since the clubhead must sweep the ball off the grass, attempt this shot only from a good lie.

At the start of the punch shot out of a divot, the hands should be ahead of the ball, which is played slightly nearer the right foot than usual. This helps keep the shot low.

Throughout the hitting area the hands should move straight toward the target. The wrists must not be permitted to roll over to the left (as demonstrated in the circled drawing).

INCORRECT

Being in a divot
doesn't mean you are in a hole

You should not become alarmed when you find your ball in a divot mark or in a bad lie in the fairway. The required shot can be played successfully. In fact, I would rather hit from a divot than from a tight lie in close-cropped grass. The shot from a divot can be played two ways. You can let the ball bounce onto the green or fly it in, depending on the situation. The run-in shot is the easier of the two, and the one you should choose unless there are obstacles in front of the green. First, select a club that is one longer than you would ordinarily need; if you are a seven-iron distance from the green hit a six-iron. Play the ball back toward the right foot. Use only a three-quarter swing, picking the club up abruptly and swinging it down on top of the ball. Thus you are hitting a punch-type shot. Finally, keep your hands square to the target well after impact. The ball will travel in a low trajectory and will run a long way after it hits. Consider the terrain in front of the green carefully, for the ball must bounce off it. The shot that lets the ball hit the green on the fly is a bit more difficult. Again choose a club one longer than you would normally use. Play the ball from the normal position between your feet, but open the blade of the club. Use a slightly outside-in swing and aim toward the left, because the ball will fade back to the right. Take a full swing and hit hard with the right hand, meanwhile making sure that the wrists do not turn over at or just after impact. The ball should get up in the air quickly and come into the green in a high, fading trajectory. The fade means that it will have backspin, so the shot will stop sharply when it lands.

Don't give up on a downhill lie

The weight (blue arrow, left) must be firmly on the left side. The backswing (solid red) is to the outside and requires a quick wrist break. At impact, however, the wrists remain firm and move the hands and club face (red planes) toward the target (right).

On a hilly course you will frequently be confronted with a full shot that must be hit from a steep, downhill lie. This is a discouraging stroke to face, especially after a good drive, and demands some marked adjustments in the swing. An open stance is necessary, with most of the weight carried on the left side. The ball should be played farther back toward the right foot than usual. Since the shot will have a fairly low trajectory, a club one higher than ordinarily called for should be used—a four-iron instead of a three-iron, for example. The blade should be opened in order to help keep the ball from being pulled off to the left. The clubhead should be swung to the outside

on the backswing, and the wrists must break very sharply. Thus the arc of the swing *(solid red)* will be considerably shorter than is conventional *(dotted line)*. On the downswing the ball should be hit very hard and, though the backswing has been a wristy one, the wrists must not be allowed to roll over at or after impact. The head must be kept extremely steady. The best advice about such steep downhill lies is to stay out of them. You often can, by planning your play of a hole properly. If a driver off the tee will leave you such a shot with a nine-iron, it might be better to hit a four-wood tee shot, and a level five-iron to the green.

A compact swing
for a low-down lie

Most weekend players find the occasional sidehill lie with the ball below the feet as threatening as if it were a hissing snake. It is a nasty shot, to be sure, but the first thing to overcome is the psychological hazard. This shot can be played successfully. One of two things is likely to happen when the ball is hit: if the club face is closed at address, the ball will be pulled to the left; if the club face is square, the ball will fade to the right. The happier of these alternatives, and the easier to hit, is the fade. The club must be gripped at the very end and the knees flexed sufficiently to bring the body about as close to the ball as it would be for a normal lie. The shot should be aimed to the left of the green. The backswing must be slow and fairly compact. I cannot overstress the importance of good balance. The weight should be kept on the heels and the head kept absolutely still throughout the swing. If the head moves to either side during the shot anything can happen—a shank, a top or even a whiff, which would unhappily force you to try the whole thing all over again. Finally, to help insure solid contact, it is necessary to stay down with the shot until well into the follow-through.

THOMAS A. CANTORE
417 HOMESTEAD DR.
UTICA, NY 13502
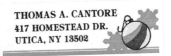

For this sidehill shot the knees should be bent and the weight firmly planted on the heels. The club is gripped at the very end and swung slowly. Since the shot will fade, it must be started to the left.

A deeper lie require

Many players, especially those with the higher handicaps, have trouble making up their minds whether to try to sweep a fairway wood shot off the grass or to punch down through the ball as they would on certain kinds of iron shots. The fact is, the shot can be played either way. The decision must be based on the lie.

On very well-kept fairways you will frequently get an exceptionally good lie for a wood shot. In this case it is possible, and more effective, to sweep the ball off the turf. The ball should be in line with the left heel at address. On the downswing you should concentrate on bringing the club face squarely into the ball at the bottom of the swing's arc. The clubhead should not dig into the grass after impact. Trying

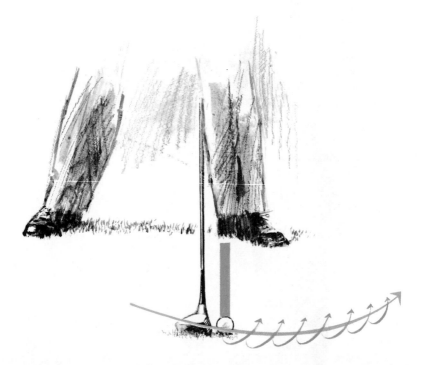

From a good lie the fairway wood is played almost as far forward as when hitting a drive. The ball is swept cleanly off the grass, and it can be hooked.

different swing

to punch down on a ball that is in a good lie will more often than not result in a shot that is blooped high in the air.

On many occasions, however, the ball will be sitting down in the grass somewhat. When this is the case the ball should be played a couple of inches nearer the right foot than usual. The club face should be open at address. This will result in a slight fade but will also help get the ball up quickly. On the downswing you should bring the club face into the ball *before* it has reached the low point of its arc. You will take turf, therefore, after the ball has been hit. By doing this you will not only get the ball up and on its way as soon as possible but also guarantee solid contact.

From a bad lie the fairway wood is used like an iron. The ball is moved toward the center of the stance, a divot is taken after contact, and the shot may fade.

Quick stop for a buried lie

When you are faced with a buried lie in a sand trap and a pin placed close to the near edge of the green you have a problem. It will be hard to stop the ball quickly enough for it to end up near the cup. The answer is to "pop" the ball out. Normally for a shot from a buried lie you must close the club face, but in this case you must open the

Open the club face wide (triangular color area).

An early wrist break sets up a deep downswing (solid area) as opposed to the path the clubhead takes on a sweeping explosion shot (dotted line).

club face wide. Then start the backswing with a very early wrist break. This brings the clubhead back on a steep, upright plane. A steep backswing naturally sets up a steep downswing. As the clubhead comes down into the impact area the right hand must completely dominate the swing. Because an open-faced club ordinarily tends to bounce off sand instead of digging into it, the right hand must drive the clubhead down into the sand with a sort of slicing action. Aim to have the clubhead enter the sand as close behind the ball as possible, while still getting it under the ball. The ball should pop right out, and have more backspin than you can get using the conventional sweeping type of explosion shot from the buried lie.

The surrounding territory often shows how a doubtful putt will break. The ball is more likely to turn with the slope of the land (solid line) than against it (dotted line).

Take time to find out
how the land lies

You are being both careful and sensible if you take time to line up your putts from both sides of the hole. Hidden breaks can often be seen by looking from the hole back toward the ball. But every now and then what you see is more confusing than enlightening. A putt will appear to break from left to right when viewed from behind the hole and from right to left when looked at from the other direction. Which angle of vision should you trust? Here is the answer: assume the putt will break in the direction that the general terrain in the area slopes. I won my first National Amateur Championship at Broadmoor, a course that is built right up against the Colorado Rockies. We all quickly learned there that the greens on the mountain side of the course invariably sloped away from the mountains, even when they appeared to slope into them. The steep terrain caused an optical illusion. What looked like an uphill putt would actually turn out to be downhill, much to the dismay of the player who hit it. To a lesser extent, this is true of all hilly or rolling courses. So—check the slope of the land around the green. If it falls off from left to right, for instance, then it is quite possible that what looks like a level putt will actually break a little from left to right. When you know your eyes are deceiving you because a putt appears to break two different ways, look beyond the green and see how the land lies.

When the lie is good (above), the ball is played off the left heel and the club face is square to the hole. Only if the lie is bad (below) is it necessary to open the club face and move the ball slightly back of the heel.

Consider the lie
before hitting the wedge

Nothing is more irritating to a golfer than to sky a wedge shot on one hole and skull it on the next. There you are within birdie range, only to make a bogey or worse. The humiliation caused by these shots is matched only by their frequency. The most common mistake on the full wedge shot is trying to hit it too hard. The result is a loss of rhythm and timing on a shot that needs a great deal of rhythm and timing. You must remember that with a wedge, the ball is caressed, not assaulted.

There are two basic ways to play the wedge shot, depending on your lie. If the ball is sitting well down in the grass, it is likely that blades of grass will get between the club face and the ball at impact. Play the ball back toward the right foot a little and open the face of the club. This will help eliminate the excessive overspin that grassy lies usually cause. You should aim the shot to the left of the hole because the ball will fade. On the downswing, bring the club through the ball at a steep enough angle to take quite a bit of turf, and use a full follow-through. The follow-through is important because in resolving to make one you will force yourself to keep the swing smooth.

If the lie is a good one, however, not much turf should be taken after impact. The ball should be played in the same position that I feel all normal iron shots should be played, somewhere opposite the left heel. (Many pros teach that the ball should be moved back toward the right foot as the irons get shorter, but I do not agree.) The backswing should be upright and made with little hip turn. The idea, above all, is to concentrate on hitting the ball solidly without rushing or forcing the swing.

Hit the shot right, and get bite

Swing firmly with the right hand, but do not let it roll over (red arrow). Moving it out toward the target (blue) will also keep the club face open and on line.

Open the club face at address (left) and take the club back at a sharp angle (blue arrow, right). Taking too flat a swing (red arrow) will cause the shot to hook, putting overspin instead of backspin on the ball.

Backspin—or bite, as it is often called—is essential for a short approach shot hit to a green that is protected by hazards in front, or when the flagstick is placed in the forward portion of the green. It is hard for a weekend player to get backspin every time he wants it, because he simply does not play enough to master this kind of shot. There are, however, certain things you can do to help produce bite. First, the lie must be a good one, so that no grass gets between the ball and the face of the club. The ball should be positioned opposite the left heel, and the club face turned open just a bit at address. The swing should be made with a slight cutting action at the point where the club head comes into the hitting area. You can do this. Don't be afraid to try it. The sharper the angle at which the clubhead comes into the ball the more backspin will be produced, so the swing should be a very upright one. Using a wedge, I pick the club practically straight up and then bring it down sharply into the back of the ball. The clubhead must be moving very fast at impact, so it is important to apply a great deal of power in the hitting zone with the right hand. It is just as vital, however, that the right hand and wrist do not roll over the left until well into the follow-through. The hands must move straight out toward the target or the ball will be hit with a closed face and all sign of bite will be yanked out of the shot.

For a rough pitch
use a gentle swing

When you miss the green with an approach shot you will often find the ball nestled in high, swirling rough. This presents a complex problem. The club must be swung hard enough to cut through a lot of deep grass before reaching the ball, yet not so hard that the ball is knocked way past the hole, or over the green.

I had experimented with many ways to hit this shot—from using a loose grip and letting the clubhead do the work, to exploding it like a sandblast—but I was never satisfied. Then, at the site of the 1961 U.S. Open, Art Wall taught me an extremely effective method. Hold on to the club very firmly with the left hand. The right hand should also grip the club tightly, but not quite as strongly as the left. Keeping the blade slightly open, take the club straight up by breaking the wrists very sharply at the start of the backswing. Then come down right on top of the ball. You should feel that you are hitting the shot with the right hand. The firm left hand will keep you from breaking your wrists too sharply at impact. Use a slow, almost lazy, swing. Take the clubhead all the way back and all the way through, but never speed up the swing. The ball will actually pop out of the rough cleanly —as it has done at left—while the clubhead continues into the grass.

This shot can be played high or low, and is most effective from 20 feet to 30 yards. Your lie in the grass and the pin position dictate how high to hit the ball. For a high shot, play the ball more off the left foot. For a low one play it more off the right.

The club should be taken up abruptly in almost a straight line by breaking the wrists very sharply at the beginning of the backswing.

At the climax of a slow, easy swing, the clubhead should come down through the ball, with the right hand firmly controlling the shot.

A delicate shot that does something no big blast can

The delicate, soft explosion shot from a trap is a difficult one for most golfers, chiefly because they approach it with great uncertainty. They are tempted to chip it, then tempted to blast it, and end up in a mental funk doing neither. Yet it is an excellent shot when you are trapped next to the green and the pin is positioned so near the trap, say within 20 feet, that you cannot play a full, conventional explosion.

It is most important to realize that this shot is not simply a reduced version of the explosion. It requires a technique entirely its own. Address the ball with a wide-open stance. Play it off the left foot, with the blade of your sand wedge turned very open. Turning the blade in this fashion brings the heavy flange more into play, encouraging the club to bounce off the sand instead of digging deep into it. Start the shot by taking the club back to the outside and on a fairly low plane. In other words, do not swing it up as abruptly as you would for the conventional explosion shot. On the downswing, hit the sand about an inch behind the ball and "skim" the ball out, taking very little sand underneath it and keeping your wrists firm on the follow-through. This will give you greater control. The skimming action is created almost automatically by the fact that you have opened up the blade at address and kept it on a low plane during the backswing. To determine how hard you should swing at this shot, imagine that it is a normal chip shot about 50% longer than the shot that faces you. One final word: be extremely careful not to move your head or body. This is one of the most exacting shots that a golfer must face. Nothing is sure to spoil it quicker than moving the head.

BACKSWING: The stance is very open. The club is kept low (solid line) and outside, compared to the normal explosion (dotted line). Swing stops at X.

DOWNSWING: Clubhead comes in from outside (solid line). Club face is open. Sand is struck an inch behind the ball, and ball is "skimmed" out.

A bold way to play

Many times in a tight tournament or a close match you will hit the ball into such an impossible lie that you just want to cry a little and walk back to the clubhouse. Please don't, because if this situation can be considered a prelude to disaster, it can also be looked on as a rare opportunity. The successful execution of such a shot can provide the psychological thrust that will unsettle your opponent or inspire you to a fast finish. One such lie occurs when your ball has rolled against the back edge of a trap in a way that makes it almost impossible to get the club head down into the ball. Ordinarily, the safest move out of this mess would be to just chip the ball firmly toward the green. If your position in the match is one in which you must gamble, however, try this. Take as steady a stance as you can under the circumstances, choke up on the club quite a bit and open its face wide. On the backswing you will have to break your wrists very sharply to get the club head up past the lip of the trap, but also take it back well to the outside of the line to the hole. The downswing will therefore be outside in, and should be made with a strong right hand. Try to make the right hand, in a sense, catch up with the left at impact. This will produce a combined cutting and scooping action that should get the ball up quickly, and maybe even near the cup.

To avoid the lip of the trap on the backswing, the club is swung back well to the outside (arrow, left) and up sharply. The right hand controls the shot.

ough **trap shot**

On a hill, stand firm and swing gently

There are two essential things to remember when hitting from a side-hill lie where the ball is higher than the feet. The first, which is obvious but surprisingly easy to forget, is that you must concentrate unusually hard on keeping your balance. The second is that the ball is probably going to hook quite a bit. To insure good balance, the player should get his weight well distributed on the heels of both feet. He should also maintain a very upright stance, with the knees flexed only slightly. Then, to counterbalance the fact that the ball will be nearer to him than usual, he should choke down on the grip of his club. Finally, the backswing should be made slowly and kept quite short; both of these things help maintain balance. At the bottom of the downswing the clubhead should not hit the ground. Instead, it should sweep the ball off the turf. If hit properly, the ball is now going to hook, so aim to the right of the hole. The shortened backswing and the choked-up grip will cut down on distance. To compensate for this it is a sound idea to use one more club (a four-iron, for instance, instead of a five) than would be used under normal circumstances.

This awkward lie requires you to shorten the backswing (red arrows), distribute weight evenly (blue) and aim to the right.

Using a wedge to avoid a risk

It is a sad fact that many good rounds are ruined by the failure of a risky shot. When faced with a situation where boldness might save a stroke, it makes sense to weigh the risk carefully against the possible gain before rushing headlong into the shot. In the U.S. Open at Oakland Hills in 1961, I was four over par after 17 holes, and on 18 I had missed the green with my approach, the ball kicking down into the rough at the left. To get the ball close to the pin, which was placed in the front right-hand corner of the green, I had an extremely delicate pitch over a deep, wide trap and a mound *(upper dotted line)*. The temptation to take the gamble and recoup some of the strokes I had lost earlier was extremely great, but so was my chance of dumping the pitch into the trap *(alternate dotted line)* and taking six or seven on the hole. I finally decided to play for a sure five and pitched the ball safely away from the trap *(solid line)*. I play these short wedge shots with an open blade and take a slow, easy swing, keeping my left hand firmly on the club and making the hit with my right hand. The idea is to get the ball up in the air quickly and have it land softly. This left me with a 15-foot putt which, as a matter of fact, I almost sank. I finished the tournament in a tie for fourth. The lesson to be learned from this is valuable, I think. In stroke play, when winning does not depend upon a particular shot, play safely away from danger and hope that a good putt will do the work for you. Sometimes you can save yourself two or three strokes this way.

To play a short wedge shot, I keep my left hand firmly on the club and direct the hit with my right hand. Using a slow, easy swing, I stroke the ball with an open blade.

The deliberately hooked low iron is a valuable shot that is especially useful on a course where there are lots of trees to be maneuvered around or under, or where there is a great deal of wind. It can be used effectively from within a short-iron distance of the green on any occasion when the ball must be kept quite low and brought into the target from right to left to avoid branches or other such obstructions.

Contrary to the general belief, it is not a hard shot to master. It should be executed with most of the weight on the left side and the ball played back toward the right foot. Aim well to the right of the target — practice will determine how much — and keep the club face at address square or slightly closed to the line of flight. Use an iron that is one lower than the distance calls for. From nine-iron distance, for example, an eight-iron should be tried, but with a three-quarter swing. The swing must be a pronounced inside-to-out one, with the clubhead taken up abruptly on the backswing and brought down into the top of the ball. The wrists should roll over naturally at impact. Using a lower club than usual and making a firm but unforced swing takes quite a bit of the excessive hook spin off the ball. The result will be a slightly hooked shot that stays low, stops reasonably quickly and is fairly easy to control; it does not run a long way, as a low hook normally would.

To produce a low hook with a short iron, the weight should be on the left side, the ball played more off the right foot, and the swing made on a pronounced inside-to-out plane (top). Only a three-quarter swing should be used, with the wrists rolling over as usual just as the ball is struck (bottom).

When to explode . .

To survive on the pro tour I've had to learn a great many shots that I was never forced to master as an amateur. One lesson I have learned is that the explosion shot can be used to advantage in more places than a sand trap. The explosion has saved me strokes on shots hit from wet turf, loose dirt, sandy rough and pine needles. It is most effective when you are in one of the above situations and have to get the ball up quickly to clear obstacles such as water, sand, bushes, mounds, etc., yet stop the ball quickly on the green. You should use either a pitching or sand wedge and address the ball with the club face wide open *(below)*. Pick the club up rather abruptly to the outside on the backswing and then come down about half an inch to an inch behind the ball, hitting the shot as if it were twice its actual length. You have to be bold,

making sure you follow through. The shot needs quite a bit of practice but the time will be very well spent. I have found putting out of a sand trap to be a good percentage shot when conditions are right. Proper conditions require a trap that is relatively flat and has little or no overhanging lip. Address the ball with your regular putting grip and stance, with this difference: play the ball off the toe of the blade *(below)* instead of the center. Most putting strokes impart backspin to the ball. Hitting it with the toe of the blade seems to give a slinging action to the putt which has a strong tendency to reduce the natural backspin and increase the possibility of a more consistent roll. It provides the control a necessarily delicate explosion shot might not and will help get the ball close to the hole.

A crisp shot for soggy sand

The ball is played off the left heel. The clubhead is kept low and the eyes are on the point where it should enter the sand, an inch behind the ball.

The backswing should be kept short, not much past waist level, and the wrists held firm on the downswing to guarantee a firm shot.

Wet sand looks like hardened cement. If you are like most golfers, when you find your ball lying in a well-soaked bunker you feel you would as soon see it on a road. Actually, you should not be alarmed, for wet sand is easier to play out of than dry sand. The reason is that the water forms an extra cushion below the ball, and the club head bounces off this cushion. This is helpful, because on this shot the club-head should not dig into the sand; it should skim through it just underneath the ball. At address, the ball should be positioned opposite the left foot and the blade of the sand wedge opened wide. The club should be swung back to the outside of the line to the target, but only about halfway back and on a low plane. On the downswing the club should enter the sand about an inch behind the ball. The open club face, the cushioning effect of the damp sand and the low plane of the swing are going to keep the clubhead from digging down too deeply. As a result, the ball will be simply nipped up and out of the sand. The longer the shot required, of course, the longer the backswing should be.

The shot from an elevated tee or fairway to a green below is one that requires more than the usual amount of thought. It is a deceptive shot that can hurt you badly if you do not think about it — and lots of golfers don't. The first thing to consider is that the ball will carry much farther than usual because the extra drop extends the parabola of the shot. How much farther? My general rule is that the shot will travel 10 feet farther than normal for each 20 feet of elevation. Take the 13th hole at the Columbus Country Club, site of the 1964 PGA Championship, for instance. This is a par 3 hole of 160 yards where the championship

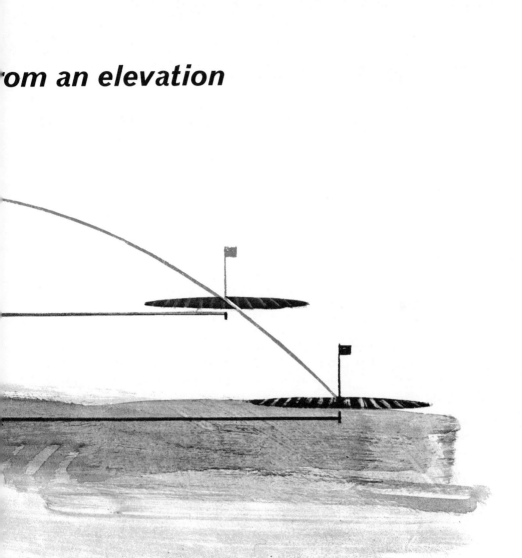

tee is right next to the regular men's tee but 40 feet higher. With no wind I find I need a firm six-iron from the regular tee, but nothing more than a smooth seven-iron from the championship tee.

A second important factor to keep in mind is that from an elevated tee the effects of the wind will always be greatly exaggerated. It becomes impossible to punch the ball under a wind blowing in your face, so wind resistance is greater than for a level shot. Conversely, the ball will be carried much farther by a tailwind, and a quartering wind will have more effect than usual because the ball is in the air longer.

Your putting stroke

is fine for the short chip

The chip shot from 5 to 15 feet off the green should be executed almost like a putt. You should always be able to get down in two strokes from such a position and occasionally in one. The stance for this shot should be open and the club choked down considerably. The hitting action nearly duplicates the putting stroke. It is made primarily with the wrists, but the wrists must break almost straight back. They must not be allowed to roll over as the ball is hit. This movement will keep the back of the left hand, and therefore the face of the club, as square as possible to the chipping line. This is an extremely important element in setting up a solid and accurate shot. On the backswing the left hand will break in under the right. On the downswing it leads the right hand and the clubhead straight out toward the hole.

You should try to land the ball about five feet into the green and allow it to roll the rest of the way to the hole. The amount of loft needed to land it on that spot and still have it roll the required distance determines what club should be used. Assuming the green is level, if the correct landing spot is approximately halfway between the ball and the hole, a nine-iron or wedge should be used. If the spot is a quarter of the way to the hole, a six- or seven-iron is the correct club.

On the backswing for the chip shot (above) the wrists
should break with a hinge-like action. This keeps the
hands, and therefore the club face, square on target. On
the follow-through (right) the left hand must stay on the
line to the hole.

THREE FEET

Stand up to
those long, long putts

The long putt is one of the hardest shots in golf. Most golfers, having very little idea of how to hit it, and nervous about the prospect, either slam the ball way past the hole or hit the putt so poorly it hardly gets halfway there. The long putt is a difficult shot for me, too, but there are several things that can be done to help eliminate three-putt greens. The player should walk up the line of the putt to examine the grass and get a better idea of the distance from the ball to the hole. Most greens have some degree of inconsistency, and the grass near the hole may, for instance, be thinner and therefore faster than the grass along the early line of the putt. I have found it is a good idea to take a more upright stance when addressing the long putt than the short putt. Doing this raises the level of the eyes and thus makes it a little easier to judge the distance up to the moment the ball is struck. It actually is more important to hit this shot solidly than with great accuracy. You are much more apt to be 10 feet short than 10 feet to the left or right. A solid hit will at least give the ball a chance to reach the area of the cup. Finally, I always visualize an imaginary circle around the hole about six feet in diameter. What I try to do is let the ball die just at the front edge of this circle. This gives me an error margin of six feet, three feet short or three feet long.

Getting the palm into the putt

An important part of my game in the U.S. Open at Oakmont in June 1962 was my putting. Even on those fast greens I was fortunate enough to three-putt only one hole of the 90 I played, and I saved several pars by getting down some tough five- and six-foot putts. I now feel that my victory was made partially possible by something I had learned the previous winter. At that time I played a practice round with Jack Burke just before the Palm Springs Desert Classic. I had been putting badly and Jack said he thought I was pulling the putter into the stroke with my fingers instead of swinging the club through with the palm of my right hand. This was not only causing me to pull putts off line, but was

also making me erratic in regard to distance. To correct this mistake in my grip, I moved my right hand to the right so that my thumb was on top of the shaft and the palm of my hand directly under it *(above left)*. I practiced with this new grip all week. The following week I discarded the light blade putter I had been using and switched to a heavier blade putter so that I could adjust my stroke more easily to the varying speeds of the greens we encounter from week to week on the tour. Since then, thanks to the new putter and a now much more solidly positioned right hand, I have been putting consistently well. I think these adjustments may help you, too.

The most frequent mistake made on the short putt is not hitting the ball firmly enough. This causes the putt to either die short of the hole, which is infuriating, or slip off to one side because the ball's slow motion lets the slope of the green or a bumpy spot have an excessive effect. If you are having short-putt trouble, check three points in your putting technique. First, you should not start choking down on the club when faced with a short putt. Doing so makes the club feel much lighter than usual and is likely to cause a jerky, uneven stroke. This is an error we all fall into. To be sure that it does not happen to me, I have made my putter grip so short that I can hold it only near the top. Second, you should concentrate on making a firm stroke, not just at impact, but after impact as well. To insure this, push the putter blade well through the ball and out toward the hole. Third, after considering the break and determining the line to the hole, you should try picking out a spot on that line, about five or six inches short of the hole, and aim the putt at it. I do this, and it seems to at least get the putt started in the right direction.

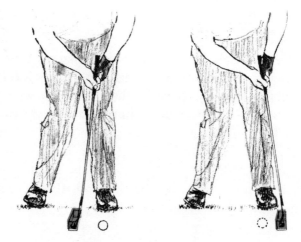

...en hit the putt firmly

Aiming at a spot along the line of the putt will help you keep the putt on line and also improve your concentration. The stroke (left) must be firm, with the head of the putter carried well through toward the hole.

ιake a pitch with a putt

Too many of us, I think, reach for a chipping or pitching club on those delicate little shots around the green that might be better executed with a putter. The playing conditions, of course, must be right. You should be playing over firm turf that is free of heavy or wet grass, and you should be in a situation in which the pin placement makes it quite difficult to get a pitch shot close—especially from a thin lie. The pin might be on the side of the green closest to you or tucked behind a mound that a pitch shot might not clear but a putt would roll over. Use your usual putting stroke on this shot. Since the ball will bounce quickly over the hard ground, you do not need to hit it much harder than a regular putt. I knew about this shot, but I seldom had occasion to play it until I came out on the tour. Now on certain courses I often use it several times a round. In the second round of the 1962 Masters, for instance, I hit a poor second shot on the 9th hole and my ball stopped 40 feet to the right of the green. The pin was on the lower right side of the green and there was a mound between the ball and the cup. Without a great deal of luck I could not have pitched the ball near the pin, so I putted it over the relatively hard surface. It went up over the mound and to within five feet of the hole. This is strictly a percentage shot that will work to your advantage in the long run. The point I wish to make is that by using a putter under these conditions you will get the ball close to the hole more often than with a lofted club; there also is less chance of wasting additional strokes.

How to concede and win

Conceding short putts in the big amateur match-play tournaments is seldom a haphazard business. My practice as an amateur was always to make my opponent putt the short ones on the first couple of holes, concede them in the middle of the match and then, when the match was tight in the closing holes, make him putt them again. The reason for this is simple. On the first two or three holes the short putts are harder because nobody has settled down. In the closing holes of a tight match, they can be harder still if you haven't had to try putting for a dozen or so holes. The hole is suddenly going to look as small as a thimble and your putter will feel about as secure in your hands as a live snake. In the finals of the 1959 North and South Amateur at Pinehurst I was playing Gene Andrews, a pretty shrewd golfer from California. It was a tight match, and we were both fighting hard to build a margin by lunchtime. The match was even on the 15th and I needed only to drop a two-foot putt for my par and a 1-up lead. But Gene, instead of conceding, just walked to the next tee. I blew the putt, and the match was still tied. I won the 16th, and on the 17th, a par 3, I had my chance. I was in the hole in par and all Gene needed was a two-footer for a half. I just stood on the edge of the green and didn't say a word. Suddenly he had to make a putt he hadn't tried all morning. He missed it, and I took a vital 2-up lead in to lunch. I certainly needed it, because I had to sink a six-foot putt on the 36th to win the match, 1 up. Elsewhere in this book I discuss a related subject — learning from your opponent's shot.

How to keep swinging
in the rain

Some people must enjoy hitting shots off wet grass—the fanatic, say, who plays so early in the morning that the dew is still thick enough to swim in or the all-weather zealot who looks upon a tropical rainstorm as nothing more than a light mist. Most of us, however, take little pleasure in such shots because they are hard to handle. The main problem is that moisture fills the grooves of the club face. This makes it difficult for the clubhead to grip the ball at impact and give it backspin. The result is a shot that flies farther than it would under normal conditions and then does not bite properly when it lands. The way to counteract this is to play a fading shot into the green. To hit this shot, one less club than normal should be used (a seven-iron, for instance, rather than a six). The ball should be aimed to the left of the target, and the swing should be made almost entirely with the arms. There should be, in other words, very little hand action at impact. The right hand should stay behind the left with the hands not turning over until well into the follow-through. The clubhead should not dig into the turf; it should sweep the ball cleanly off the grass. The result will be a high shot that still carries farther than normal, but one that will hold the green when it lands.

The arms control this swing. Hand action is limited and the ball is hit cleanly, as if being swept off a steel plate.

There are times for caution in match play

Ideally in match play you should compete against the course and not your opponent, but there are many times when you must check your opponent's position, and the percentages, before proceeding. Quite likely this will keep you from doing something foolish. My only match-play loss of 1961 was due, mainly, to a stubborn disregard of percentages. In the first round of that year's Colonial Amateur Invitational in Memphis I was leading Bobby Greenwood of North Texas State 1 up with three holes to play. On the 520-yard 16th I had driven into the left rough, but he then put his second shot into a trap up near the green. I thought, aha, I'll just knock the ball onto the green with a one-iron, win the hole and be 2 up with two holes to play. To do so I had to hit a 220-yard shot out of the rough and over two traps that guarded the left side of this very firm green. The smart play would have been to hit a three-iron safely *(dotted line)* to the front of the green and chip from there for my birdie. I certainly would have had a much better chance of getting down in 2 from there than my opponent did from the trap. But I smashed away with the one-iron just the same *(solid line)* and wound up burying the ball under the lip of the first trap. I was lucky to get a 5, but still lost the hole to Greenwood's birdie. As a result, when I won the 17th it merely put me 1 up again instead of closing out the match 2 and 1. When Greenwood eagled the 18th and birdied the first extra hole I was beaten. The golfing moral is clear: when your opponent is in trouble and you've got a lead with only a couple of holes to play, don't get greedy. You may go hungry instead.

Knowing a small rule
can be a great help

A thorough knowledge of golf rules can be of great help to you, because there are times when a regulation that seems to restrict the player actually aids him. An example is Paragraph 22-2c of *The Rules of Golf,* which concerns dropping or placing the ball after a free or penalty lift. It is a rule that comes up frequently in tournament play, and I have benefited by it more than once since joining the pro tour. The rule reads:

"If a dropped ball rolls out of bounds, into a hazard or more than two club-lengths from the point of dropping, it may be re-dropped, without penalty. If the configuration of the ground makes it impossible to prevent the ball from so rolling, it may be placed at the point of dropping."

The rule clearly states that if the ball rolls into one of the three situations you are allowed to redrop it without penalty, but it implies something equally as important. If the ball rolls into a more favorable

spot (provided it does not end up any nearer the hole), you are also allowed to play it from there.

Here is an example from one of my competitive experiences to illustrate what I mean. During the third round of the 1962 Crosby I was playing the Pebble Beach course and at the 5th hole, a 160-yard par 3, I embedded my tee shot in the dirt alongside a sand trap fronting the green. From this spot, even if the ball had not been embedded, I would have had an extremely delicate pitch over the trap. But under a PGA tournament ruling I was allowed a free drop because the ball *was* embedded. Since the ground sloped to the left, when I dropped the ball it rolled away from the trap—but not nearer the hole—and left me with an easy shot. Thanks to Rule 22-2c, I was allowed to play the ball from this spot and chipped it up close for my par.

If you are one of the many golfers with small hands, try the interlocking grip. There is a good chance you will discover that it fuses your hands together and holds them on the club much more securely than the popular overlapping grip. My hands are small and the interlocking grip is the one I use today, but a few years ago, in an experimental mood, I fooled around with the overlap and the baseball grips. I played some 50 rounds using the overlap, but my hands always felt as if they were flying apart. This was particularly so just before impact. My trial

For the overlap grip, I place the little finger of my right hand over my left between the index and middle fingers.

In the baseball grip, which I once gave a short trial, all ten fingers are placed directly on the club.

with the baseball grip was even briefer. I was able to take a good, firm hold on the club, but my hands seemed to be working against each other in different directions. In each case I was unable to maintain proper control of my swing. I gave up my experiments and have stayed with the interlocking grip ever since. It gives my hands a wonderful feeling of unity throughout the swing, a unity that the other grips could not supply. If you have small hands, too, I think you will find that the interlocking grip will work as well for you as it does for me.

Using the interlocking grip, I lift the index finger of my left hand off the shaft and intertwine it with the little finger of my right. I have comparatively small hands, and this has proved to be my best method for controlling the club.

A pregame warmup is important in all sports but possibly more so in golf because the action, undertaken from a stationary position, gives the muscles such a sudden, violent wrench. If you are to hit good golf shots, your muscles must be properly prepared. I start my warmup by using a wedge for the trio of exercises shown here. These are designed not only to give the hands a sense of "feel" but also to limber up the wrist, forearm and upper and lower back muscles. No player should tee off without some such warming-up routine.

Most golfers do not have the time or the facilities to hit any practice shots prior to playing; but, when it is possible, here is a sensible system to follow after the initial warmup. Begin by hitting a few wedge shots, then use the eight-iron, the five-iron, the two-iron, the three-wood and finish up with the driver. It is better, when time is limited, to hit the eight-iron six times than to hit the nine, eight and seven twice each. Conclude your preround preparations with some chipping and putting at the practice green.

Hold the club as above and rotate body back and forth from hips up, to loosen the upper back and shoulder muscles.

To stretch the lower back muscles, hook the club through elbows and again rotate body back and forth from hips up.

Swing a wedge back and forth with a wristy motion to give the hands "touch" and loosen the wrist and forearm muscles.

STIFF   **REGULAR**   **WHIPPY**   **STIFF OR
EXTRA STIFF**

Club flexibility

The flexibility of club shafts is usually rated in four categories; A for whippy, R for regular, S for stiff, and X for extra stiff. Or as my company, MacGregor, does it; 3 for whippy, 2 for regular, 1 for stiff and X for extra stiff. When a golfer buys a new set of clubs he will find that this rating applies to every club in the set. For the week-end player, greater whippiness will produce greater distance, but at the cost of accuracy. In general, if you are between 13 and 35 years old and break 90 you can function best with the "3" shaft, but each player must decide for himself what he needs and prefers. There is one way, however, for a fussy player to come up with an excellent combination of shafts. My former golf coach at Ohio State, Bob Kepler, is one who employs this ingenious system. He figures that his long irons must supply distance, his short irons accuracy. In his woods he uses stiff shafts but on his long irons (Nos. 2 and 3) he has a whippy A shaft. With this shaft he is able to get more distance and a higher trajectory on his shots. In his middle irons (Nos. 4-6) he uses an R shaft and in his short irons, which need not be long but must be accurate, he uses an S shaft. This is a very sound idea, though not many weekend golfers are going to be in a position to have clubs hand-tailored in this fashion. I myself employ a variation on Kepler's theme. I have had an X shaft taken from a driver, cut down, and put in my pitching wedge.

A time to
hit from the left side

The need for a left-handed golf shot (by a right-handed golfer) occurs more often and on more critical occasions than most golfers think. It is a good shot to know, I can tell you, as I have had to make several left-handed shots in my golfing career. Once, at a key point in an early-round match with Truman Connell during the 1960 Colonial Amateur Invitational in Memphis, I was 1 up after 12 holes. On the 13th, a 500-yard par 5, I drove the ball off line to the right about two inches from the side of a tree; I had a good lie, but it was impossible to do anything right-handed except chip the ball a few feet. So I turned my five-iron upside down *(see small drawing)*, swung left-handed and managed to hit the ball 150 yards down the fairway just 70 yards short of the green. I birdied the hole with a wedge and a short putt, eventually won this close match 2 and 1 and went on to win the tournament.

For this peculiar type of shot, employ a standard left-hand grip (in other words, your usual grip reversed) and swing left-handed, just trying to make sure you hit the ball. I favor using a five-, six- or seven-iron and turning it over so that you will hit the ball with the face of the club, not the back of it. These clubs are best, because they give you plenty of club face. They also can be adjusted—upside down—to supply any amount of loft you want. The next time you are on the practice tee, try some left-handed shots. A few moments of this practice will someday prove valuable to you in the course of play.

Reverse the grip for a left-handed shot, turn the club face over, and hit the ball with the face of the club.

Watch, learn and punch

When you are in the fortunate position of being able to watch an opponent hit to the green first, whether in match or stroke play, be alert to take full advantage of the opportunity. Try to determine what club he is using, observe the flight of the ball and what happens to it when it lands. It was just such close attention to Charlie Coe's approach shot to the very last green that helped me win the 1959 National Amateur at Broadmoor. On the 36th hole of our final-round match both Charlie and I had driven perfectly. I was six feet ahead of him, however, so it was up to him to hit first. Using an eight-iron, Charlie hit what appeared to be an excellent shot right at the pin, placed at the rear of the green. But the ball didn't take well on the unexpectedly hard green, and it bounded over the back edge. I actually had an eight-iron in my hand too before I saw how hard the green was. I put it away and switched to a nine-iron. With this club I hit a low punch shot, playing the ball to land on the front of the green and roll to the back. It did exactly that, stopping eight feet from the cup. To play this punch-and-run shot correctly the ball should be positioned back near the right foot. The face of the blade should be square to the target and kept that way as much as possible throughout the swing. At impact the hands do not roll over but lead the club through and out toward the target. Charlie hit a beautifully delicate little pitch back that almost went into the cup, but I then proceeded to hole my eight-footer and win the championship. If I had been first to hit to the green, or had not paid such close attention to Charlie's shot, the result probably would have been different.

Following through on a punched short-iron shot, the hands do not roll over but move out toward target.

Straight left arm at address

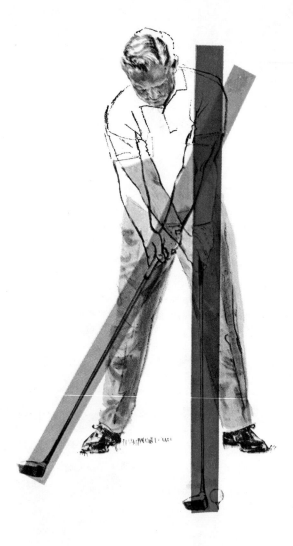

If the hands are ahead of the ball at address
(red vertical line), the club can be drawn
back keeping the same relationship on the
backswing (slanted line).

One of the intriguing facts of the golf swing is that a player will usually duplicate at impact the position he was in at address. Linked with this is the fundamental idea that the hands should be slightly ahead of the ball at impact, thus leading the clubhead through the ball and out toward the target. The obvious conclusion? At address you should set yourself up so that your hands are ahead of the ball, not opposite it or behind it. This will not only aid in achieving good position at impact, it will make it possible to start the club, the hands and the arms back simultaneously in a firm, controlled swing.

A good way to make sure that you can consistently be in the proper address position is to take your stance and then place your hands in such a way that a straight line could be drawn (as at left) from the clubhead, up through the left hand and to the left shoulder.

At impact, the hands once again lead the clubhead through the ball.

The way to a steady head is through the feet

When I was a boy just learning to play golf under Jack Grout at the Scioto Country Club in Columbus, Ohio, one of the first things he taught me was the importance of keeping my head still during the swing. This is a very difficult thing for beginners to learn, and the method used with me is the best I have ever encountered. It involves, oddly enough, the feet.

Mr. Grout made me hit hundreds—maybe even thousands—of five-iron shots before I was allowed to start hitting woods at all, and here is what I was practicing. I would take my stance and plant my heels solidly on the ground. Then I would hit the five-iron, trying not to lift either foot. It was simply a flat-footed swing. On the backswing I would roll the left ankle in toward the right, and on the downswing roll the right ankle toward the left. The inside edge of each shoe would bite into the ground, but my feet would remain stationary. What this did was keep me squarely over the ball and make it almost impossible for me to shift my body or head. Now, as the beginner progresses, he can gradually lift his left heel off the ground as the club goes back and turn the right foot up onto the toes during the follow-through and still be able to keep his head steady throughout the swing.

Both feet should remain completely on the ground throughout the practice shot. At the top of the backswing (above) the left ankle will turn in, but the heel should not be raised. In the follow-through (right) the right ankle will turn, but again the heel should not rise.

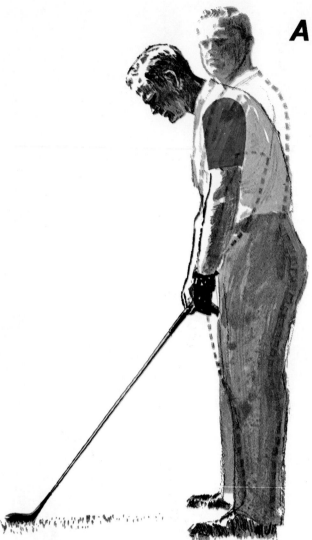

At address your hands and arms should be as nearly as possible in the position you would like them to be at impact. This duplication is difficult to achieve if your hands at address are placed either too close to your body or are straining to reach a ball that is too far away. If you don't bend just the right amount, you are in trouble.

There is a routine I follow to help me consistently keep the proper distance. First, I stand upright, with my shoulders in their natural

fatal case of the bends

position. Then I flex my knees a little and relax my shoulders, letting them slump forward. This pulls my head down and inclines the upper body toward the ball. Finally, I grip the club and extend it out directly behind the ball, keeping in mind that I want my left arm, left hand and the shaft of the club to form a line that dips only slightly away from the plane between my left shoulder and the clubhead. By starting from this position, I am able to take a swing that is free enough for me to keep my arms flowing easily past my body as I come down. I am also well balanced, because I will not have to lurch forward and reach for the ball.

Stand straight up (left, dotted line), with your club held loosely, then slump the shoulders before moving the club out to meet the ball. At the proper address position (right), the arms and the club shaft form a slight angle.

*A good way to quiet the nerves in a tough
situation is to take extra practice swings.*

When the tension builds up
—slow down

Tension can be such a terrifying thing that you can get scared just thinking about getting into a position where it can hit you—like leading a tournament or being on the verge of breaking 70 for the first time. When you get tense you stop playing and start praying—praying that bad luck will befall everyone else in the field or that extraordinary good fortune will suddenly come your way. Actually, there is no reason to succumb to tension. With a little thought and a little self-control it can be overcome or even made to work for you.

In a tense situation many golfers will rush into their shots, probably on the grounds that what must be done is best done quickly. They cannot stand the suspense. This is a mistake that will automatically result in a bad shot. At critical moments a player feeling pressure should step back, take a deep breath and enjoy the challenge, not evade it. Properly controlled, this tension can actually help you hit a better-than-usual shot.

It is also common for a golfer with a chance to accomplish something special in his career to convince himself that he is playing over his head, that his success cannot last. Well, of course, it can last, so save such post-mortem thoughts for the clubhouse. Tell yourself that your worries are ridiculous, that you have played well so far and that there is no reason why you cannot keep it up for the last few holes. It is your day.

Finally, one of the first things tension can destroy is the tempo or smoothness of your swing. Under pressure, therefore, make a special effort to concentrate on maintaining your tempo. One good way to do this is to take an extra practice swing or two, thus reestablishing the rhythm so necessary for golf success.

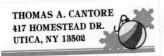

THOMAS A. CANTORE
417 HOMESTEAD DR.
UTICA, NY 13502